The Soul in Balance

The Gardens of Washington National Cathedral

*Happy 40
to my best
friend —
Love,
Jul
02*

Photographs by Alexandra Korff Scott ✤ *Texts Chosen by Heddy Fairbank Reid*

New Testament Texts Chosen by Isabelle Scott

EPM Publications, Inc.

Delaplane, Virginia

Library of Congress Cataloging-in-Publication Data

Scott, Alexandra K.
        The soul in balance : the gardens of the Washington National
Cathedral / photography by Alexandra K. Scott : texts chosen by
Heddy F. Reid.
            p. cm.
        ISBN 1-889324-11-6
            1. Washington National Cathedral Gardens (Washington, D.C.)—
Pictorial works. 2. Church gardens—Washington (D.C.)—Pictorial
works. I. Reid, Heddy. II. Washington National Cathedral
(Washington, D.C.) III. Title.
        SB466.U65W3837 1998
        712'.7'09753—dc21
                                                            98-6337
                                                            CIP

EPM Publications, Inc., 4138 Fox Hollow Road, Delaplane, Virginia 220144

Cover and book design by Tom Huestis

Third printing 2000

Permissions

The Henri-Frédéric Amiel quotation was used as a blessing at Saint Alban's Church, Washington, DC, during Advent, 1997.

Paul Caponigro quotation reprinted with permission from *Meditations in Light*, by Paul Caponigro. Santa Fe: © 1996, the Morris Press.

Willa Cather quotation reprinted with permission from: *Death Comes for the Archbishop*, by Willa Cather. New York: Alfred A. Knopf, Inc. © 1927 by Willa Cather, renewed 1995 by the Executors of the Estate of Willa Cather.

Robert Frost quotation from: *The Poetry of Robert Frost*, edited by Edward Connery Lathem, ©1975 by Lesley Frost Ballantine, Copyright 1947, © 1969 by Henry Holt and Company, Inc. Reprinted by permission of Henry Holt and Company.

Dag Hammarskjöld quotation reprinted with permission from *Markings*, by Dag Hammarskjöld. New York: © 1964, Random House, Inc.

David Ignatow "Hard Earth," from *David Ignatow: Poems 1934-1969*, © 1970 by David Ignatow, Wesleyan University Press. Reprinted by permission of University Press of New England.

St. John of the Cross quotation reprinted with permission from *The Collected Works of St. John of the Cross*, translated by Kieran Kavanaugh and Otilio Rodriguez, © 1979, 1991, by Washington Province of Discalced Carmelites. ICS Publications, Washington, DC.

Kenneth Leech quotation reprinted with permission from *True Prayer, an Invitation to Christian Spirituality*, by Kenneth Leech. Harrisburg: © 1995, Morehouse Publishing.

Henri Nouwen quotation reprinted with permission from: *Show Me the Way*, by Henri J.M. Nouwen, © 1993 by Darton, Longman, & Todd, Ltd., London.

Theodore Roethke quotation reprinted with permission from: *The Collected Poems of Theodore Roethke*, by Theodore Roethke. New York: © 1975, Doubleday Anchor Books.

Barbara Brown Taylor quotation reprinted with permission from *The Preaching Life*, by Barbara Brown Taylor. Cambridge: © 1993, Cowley Publications.

The Soul in Balance

Contents

Authors' Note

The Soul in Balance grew out of a collaboration born of a deep friendship. Alexandra K. Scott took the luminous photographs of the Cathedral gardens that are the foundation of this work; Heddy Reid, whose concept it was to pair the images with the words, chose most of the quotations and photographs and knit the book together in its present form; Isabelle Scott, who had the original vision of doing a book together, wove into it the New Testament texts and photographs. The final outcome reflects the joyous labor of three people.

Acknowledgments

We are deeply grateful to the Very Reverend Nathan D. Baxter, Dean of Washington National Cathedral, for writing the Preface. Canon Margot Semler gladdened our hearts with her enthusiasm and early support. Dennis Braden, of the Cathedral Museum Shop Bookstore, and Robert Becker, Director of Public Affairs at the Cathedral, also offered us strong support for this book.

We would particularly like to acknowledge Polly Mitchell of All Hallows Guild, whose in-depth knowledge and long years of dedication to the Cathedral gardens were invaluable to us. She wrote the Introduction, advised us from the early stages of this book, and expertly edited the Botanical Notes. We are grateful also to Joanne Murphy for her thoughtful work on the Garden History; to Julie White, President of All Hallows Guild, for her help and support; and to Laura Felt, Kay Brown, and their colleagues at the Herb Cottage for their enthusiastic advocacy of this project.

We acknowledge with special thanks Eliza Scott, our unofficial literary agent, for her professional expertise and advice, her enthusiasm, and her help in the preparation of our book proposal.

We would like to thank our wonderful publisher, Evelyn P. Metzger, for making our project a reality. Her professionalism, excitement about the book, and sense of humor have been a constant pleasure. Tom Huestis, book designer *extraordinaire*, understood exactly what we wanted and knew how to achieve it.

Finally, we acknowledge with gratitude the patience and fortitude of Hugh Scott and Trip Reid, who helped us in too many ways to count, and contributed to *The Soul in Balance* with their minds, their eyes, and their hearts.

Preface

The Very Reverend Nathan D. Baxter
Dean of Washington National Cathedral

We learn from the Book of Genesis that the earth, in its original and pristine form, was created by God as a garden. I think that most people who spend some time close to nature sense there a kind of primal comfort and inspiration that can be found in no other setting. The gardens of Washington National Cathedral offer not only an aesthetic pleasure to visitors each year, but also an experience by which they are reminded of God's first vision for the world. Many people find inspiration and renewal here.

We hope that *The Soul in Balance*, with its exquisite photographs and evocative texts, will offer you a vision of the splendor of God's creation on earth. The peace and beauty to be found in the Cathedral grounds are reflected throughout these pages. I believe this book will bless a great many hearts.

Introduction

I first met Sandy Scott fifteen years ago when she used to take pictures as she walked her dog in the Cathedral close. I was struck by her sensitivity to the seasonal beauty of the gardens, often revealing the mystery of God's handiwork by reflecting the wonder of nature. Captured in a botanical kaleidoscope of the Christian year were snowdrops nestling in the winter snows, followed by the exuberant spring tulips blending into the fragrant roses and herbs of summer, finally dissolving into the vibrant euonymus of autumn. An oft-heard comment in those days was: "I know the Cathedral, but did not know about the gardens."

Thus began a fourteen-year project entitled "Gardens of Washington National Cathedral," a calendar devoted to sharing with the general public the early vision of Bishop Satterlee, Frederick Law Olmsted, Jr., and Florence Brown Bratenahl. They foresaw the creation of gardens suitable for a fourteenth century Gothic cathedral: ancient, walled gardens appealing to the five senses, filled with plants of historic interest, plants of biblical myth and legend, and native plants. Tranquil,

permanent, and timeless: hallowed yet real, set in the midst of a bustling capital city.

Those of us who have spent time in the gardens have found that they offer us comfort and renewal. A continuum with the past, present, and future of our lives, they bestow upon us a sense of sanctuary and well-being typical of medieval gardens. Rites of passage embedded in a seasonal liturgy help us to accept the eternal fact of the mystery of life and death. One could not ask for more in a recreated paradise.

Visitors to the Cathedral close cannot help but leave with a new perspective born of the inspiration that comes from one of life's moving experiences. No matter what time of year or time of day, this outdoor sanc-

All Hallows Guild celebrated its eightieth anniversary in 1996, a remarkably long and faithful stewardship. Such devotion seems rare in a world of fads and whimsies, yet the Guild has remained true to its original task, the care and beautification of the Cathedral close. I have no doubt that it will continue to do so in the years to come.

—POLLY MITCHELL

Polly Mitchell

Past President, All Hallows Guild

tuary presents something different but special to each of us in our moments of joy, anger, even cynicism. Perhaps that is because it reflects God's loving presence in the world to forgive, reconcile, and heal. We are reminded in the Book of Genesis: And they heard the sound of the Lord God walking in the garden in the cool of the day.

In 1997 poet Heddy Reid suggested pairing some of her favorite calendar pictures with carefully chosen quotes. Her sensitive texts caught the spirit of the gardens and enhanced the meaning of these lovely photographs. Garden docents often remark that it is meaningful to hear and read what others have to say about this magical place. It is a privilege to share this spiritual journey with so many people, and to know that long after we are gone, others will follow in our footsteps.

The History of the Washington National Cathedral Gardens

The Bishop's Garden, lawn, and Woods of Washington National Cathedral are part of the 57-acre close, or outdoor area, surrounding the Cathedral on Mount Saint Alban in Washington, D.C. As ground was broken for construction of the Cathedral in 1907, Frederick Law Olmsted, Jr., of the firm responsible for New York City's Central Park, was appointed landscape architect, a post he held until 1928.

Henry Yates Satterlee, the first Episcopal Bishop of Washington, had obtained the land for the Cathedral in 1898. Joseph Nourse, Registrar of the U.S. Treasury, was an earlier landowner who purchased the land in 1813 and named it Mount Saint Alban. Some plants in the garden date to his time.

From the beginning, and with admirable foresight, the Protestant Episcopal Cathedral Foundation Park Board chose to pay attention to the importance of the gardens' development. Even before ground was broken in 1907, Beatrix Jones Farrand, the first American woman landscape architect, served as landscaping consultant. Then, in 1916, Florence Brown Bratenahl, wife of the Cathedral's dean, founded All Hallows Guild to "provide for the care and beautification of the Cathedral gardens and grounds."

Mrs. Bratenahl first focused her attention and that of the Guild on the Bishop's Garden. She led a fundraising campaign, making a large personal donation, and in 1925 had the money to begin development of the garden around Olmsted's plan. After Olmsted left in 1928, Mrs. Bratenahl served as the Cathedral's landscape designer until 1936. The Bishop's Garden offers a series of beautiful vistas. There are two perennial borders, three herb gardens, and an extensive rose garden that blooms from May to November.

The garden is full of history, from the Shadow House, built with stones from President Cleveland's summer home, to plants that came from private gardens in the area, including Hayfield Manor, once owned by George Washington, and Thomas Jefferson's Monticello. The Aquia Creek quarry in Stafford County, Virginia, provided stone for the 51 Pilgrim Steps that take the visitor from the Pilgrim Road to the Cathedral's south portal. The stone was also used for enclosing the Bishop's Garden. Stone from quarries in the same area was used by George Washington for the foundations of Mount Vernon and for the U.S. Capitol.

Adding to the gardens' historic impact, artifacts from the medieval world are found throughout its many "rooms." There is a ninth century baptismal font in the Hortulus, or "little garden," surrounded

by herbs found on a plant list drawn up by Charlemagne in 812 A.D. Bas-relief sculptures of saints are set into several of the walls that define the perimeters of the garden, and a pilgrim cross stands as a sentinel in the upper perennial border.

Much of the responsibility for the Bishop's Garden remains with All Hallows Guild, which continues to supervise all landscape design and provides the capital budget for planting and replanting, as well as for the services of landscape architects, arborists, and tree maintenance experts.

In 1996 the Guild celebrated its eightieth anniversary, and added another project as an extension of its mission: restoration of the Olmsted Woods, which lie south of the Bishop's Garden. The Woods encompass the last wooded area of the close, which was originally oak and beech forest. Over five years the Guild will finance, through donations, an extensive revitalization of the Woods, where George Washington is reputed to have ridden horseback in the late eighteenth century.

— ALL HALLOWS GUILD

11

In loving memory of

Nicholas T. Reid
September 22, 1966 - August 24, 1972

Alexander Korff Scott
July 16, 1970 - July 30, 1992

Let nothing disturb you,
Let nothing dismay you.
All things pass:
God never changes.

—SAINT TERESA OF AVILA
(1515-1582)

The world will never starve for want of wonders,
but only for want of wonder.

—G.K. CHESTERTON
(1874 - 1936)

Be still and cool in thy own mind and spirit.

—GEORGE FOX
(1624-1691)

God Almighty first planted a garden.
And indeed it is the purest of all human pleasures.

—SIR FRANCIS BACON
(1561-1626)

You have changed my sadness into a joyful dance;
You have taken away my sorrow
And surrounded me with joy.

—PSALM 30:11

...ahead of them went the star...
until it stopped over the place
where the child was.
When they saw that the star had stopped,
they were overwhelmed with joy.

— MATTHEW 2:9-10

...you are being rooted and grounded in love.

—EPHESIANS 3:17

*The Lord will cover you with his feathers
and under his wings you will find refuge.*

—PSALM 91:4

The seed of God is in us.
Given an intelligent and hardworking farmer,
it will thrive and grow up into God, whose seed
it is; and accordingly its fruits will be God-nature.
Pear seeds grow into pear trees, nut seeds into
nut trees, and God seeds into God.

—MEISTER ECKHART
(1260-1329)

I have always known
that at last I would take this road,
but yesterday
I did not know that it would be today.

—ARIWARA NO NARIHIRA
9TH CENTURY JAPAN

What you do may seem insignificant,
but it is very important that you do it.

—MAHATMA GANDHI
(1869-1948)

A poor widow came and put in
two copper coins
which are worth a penny.
Then he called his disciples and said to them,
"Truly I tell you,
this poor widow has put in more
than all of those...
For all of them have contributed out of their abundance;
but she out of her poverty
has put in everything she had..."

—MARK 12:42-44

So again Jesus said to them...
"I am the gate."

—JOHN 10:7-9

You shall go out with joy
and be led forth with peace.

—ISAIAH 55:12

Were there no God, we would be in this glorious world with grateful hearts and no one to thank.

—CHRISTINA ROSSETTI

(1830-1894)

God does not die on the day when we cease to believe in a personal deity, but we die on the day when our lives cease to be illuminated by the steady radiance, renewed daily, of a wonder, the source of which is beyond all reason.

—DAG HAMMARSKJÖLD
(1905-1961)
"MARKINGS"

Prayer is not an idle occupation. It's a very powerful instrument of our work and love.

—SAINT JULIAN OF NORWICH
(1342-c.1416)

To pray is to open oneself to the possibility of sainthood,
to the possibility of becoming set on fire by the Spirit.
In one of the sayings of the Desert Fathers,
a disciple asked Abbot Joseph what more could be done
than the keeping of "a modest rule."
The old man rose, lifting his hands against the sky,
and his fingers became like ten flaming torches.
He cried, "If thou wilt, thou shall be made wholly flame."

—KENNETH LEECH
"TRUE PRAYER—AN INVITATION TO CHRISTIAN SPIRITUALITY."

How far are you from me, O Fruit?
I am hidden in your heart, O Flower.

— RABINDRANATH TAGORE

(1861-1941)

And everything comes to One
As we dance on, dance on, dance on.

—THEODORE ROETHKE
"WHAT SHALL I TELL MY BONES?"

I must also be willing to look between things and not always at them, since a direct gaze often misses what may be glimpsed at the corner of the eye. The space between two branches may become more promising than the branches themselves...

—BARBARA BROWN TAYLOR
"THE PREACHING LIFE"

Say Yes when nobody asked.

—Lao Proverb

58

*Life is short and we do not have too much time
to gladden the hearts of those who travel with us,
so be swift to love and make haste to be kind.*

—HENRI-FRÉDÉRIC AMIEL
(1821-1881)

In his anguish
he prayed more earnestly
and his sweat
became like
great drops of blood
falling on the ground.

—LUKE 22:44

It would be very good if we could wake up before we die.

—Hindu Saying

*The soul that walks in love
neither tires others nor grows tired.*

—SAINT JOHN OF THE CROSS
(1542-1591)

66

*Recording the light of the outer subject
can be linked with gaining access to one's inner light.*

—PAUL CAPONIGRO
"MEDITATIONS IN LIGHT"

He who sees the infinite in all things
sees God.

—WILLIAM BLAKE
(1757-1827)

Only that day dawns to which we are awake.

—HENRY DAVID THOREAU

(1817-1862)

There is another world, but it is in this one.

—PAUL ELUARD
(1895-1952)

What counts is being attentive at all times to the voice of God's love inviting us to obey, that is, to listen with an attentive heart.

—HENRI NOUWEN
"SHOW ME THE WAY"

The world is filled with the Absolute.
To see this is to be made free.

—TEILHARD DE CHARDIN
(1881-1955)

Above all, clothe yourselves with love,
which binds everything together in perfect harmony.

—COLOSSIANS 3:14

Miracles seem to me to rest not so much upon faces
or voices or healing power coming suddenly near us from afar off,
but upon our perceptions being made finer, so that for a moment
our eyes see and our ears can hear what there is about us always.

—WILLA CAIHER
(1873-1947)
"DEATH COMES FOR THE ARCHBISHOP"

Suffering passes. Having suffered never passes.

—CHARLES PÉGUY
(1873-1914)

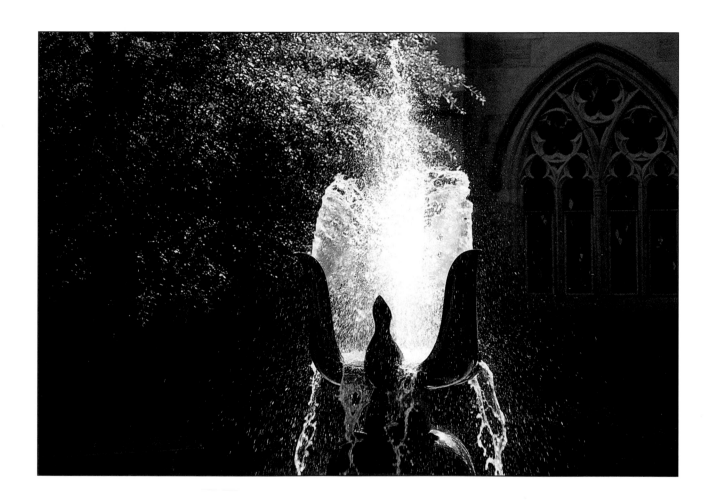

*H*ere are your waters and your watering place.
Drink and be whole again beyond confusion.

—ROBERT FROST
(1874-1963)
"DIRECTIVE"

Earth hard to my heels
bear me up like a child
standing on its mother's belly.
I am a surprised guest to the air.

—DAVID IGNATOW
"EARTH HARD"

And lo, I am with you alway,
even unto the end of the world.

—MATTHEW 28:20

With all your science, can you tell how it is, and where it is, that light comes into the soul?

—HENRY DAVID THOREAU
(1817-1862)

Botanical Notes

Cover

The pale flowers of the hardy amaryllis (*Lycoris squamigera*) add their scent to the hushed mists of summer, accenting the loving embrace of the Prodigal Son statue.

Title Page

". . .when all at once I saw a crowd, a host, of golden daffodils. . ." wrote William Wordsworth. Sometimes called Lent Lilies, they brighten the wooded south slope.

Page 8

(*top*) Laburnum, (*bottom*) Glastonbury Thorn.

Page 9

(*top*) Rhododendron austrinum, (*bottom*) Fifteenth century Gothic bas-relief.

Page 10

Bishop's Garden seen from the Cathedral tower.

Page 11

Column capital in the garth, or medieval enclosed garden.

Page 14

Stately oaks and the west facade of the Cathedral Church of St. Peter and St. Paul, better known as Washington National Cathedral, continue to share this heritage of Mount Saint Alban.

Page 16

Named after *Paeon*, the god of healing, the peony was used for medicinal purposes in the ancient world. The wild peony (*Paeonia officinalis*) of Biblical times was thought to be of divine origin and a protector of shepherds and their flocks.

Page 18

Buds of the Star magnolia (*Magnolia stellata*) stir beneath their cover of snow.

Page 20

Roses in the Bishop's Garden put on a spectacular autumnal display during Indian summer. Floribundas mixed in with the hybrid tea roses provide fragrance, adding to the enjoyment of the garden by blind visitors.

Page 22

Weeping crabapple trees shelter narcissus and muscari at the woodland's edge along the Pilgrim Road.

Page 24

A welcome sign of spring: the Star magnolia (*Magnolia stellata*) blooming on bare branches near the Pilgrim Road.

Page 26

Legendary medicinal and culinary herbs grow within the boxwood walls of the ninth century Hortulus. Fragrant rosemary (*Rosmarinus officinalis* 'Arp'), herb of remembrance originally from the Mediterranean, encircles the Carolingian baptismal font.

Page 28

Woolly betony (*Stachys byzantina*), known as lamb's ears because of its soft, furry leaves, came to the new world from Turkey and southwest Asia.

Page 30

The rare medlar (*Mespilus germanica*) was mandated in the ninth century by Charlemagne for his royal gardens, and reached the height of popularity in the Middle Ages. A native of northern Europe, it was cultivated in monastery gardens where the fruits, when fully ripened, were eaten raw or cooked for jams and tarts.

Page 32

"(The woods') extent. . . at the very crest of the slopes it clothes, (is) such as to make its sylvan quietude and its suggestion of the venerable age and enduring life of a natural forest an element of very great esthetic value. . ." Frederick Law Olmsted, Jr., 1939.

Page 34

What better enticement to the Tiger swallowtail butterfly than the clustered flowers of the butterfly bush (*Buddleia Davidii 'White Bouquet'*) in a Bishop's Lawn border?

Page 36

Colorful witch alder (*Fothergilla gardenii*) abounds in the Phyllis Nitze memorial garden. Named after the English physician, John Fothergill, this member of the witch hazel family is native to the Appalachians from Virginia to Georgia.

Page 38

This memorial replica of the original twelfth-century Norman Arch commemorates the opening of the Bishop's Garden to the public.

Page 40

The old English sundial atop a thirteenth-century capital and the Belgian granite Prodigal Son statue serve as constant companions to the tender perennials anise hyssop (*Agastache anethiodora*) and rosemary (*Rosmarinus officinalis 'Arp'*).

Page 42

The sun's rays capture the unfurling petals of *grandiflora Rosa 'Lagerfeld'* turning silvery lavender into morning blush. Named for the French fashion house, it was planted in 1986.

Page 44

The ginkgo (*Ginkgo biloba*), one of the oldest tree species on earth, is often referred to as a "living fossil." It co-existed with dinosaurs during the Mesozoic period, and owes its survival to immunity to disease and resistance to insects.

Page 46

The white flowers of *Anemone japonica* dance on long stems before a fifteenth-century bas-relief from the Gothic collection of George Gray Bernard.

Page 48

Euonymus alata 'compacta' is a native of eastern Asia. It recalls the burning bush of Exodus which Moses saw on Mount Horeb in the wilderness.

Page 50

A memorial weeping cherry (*Prunus subhirtella 'Pendula'*) frames the south transept of the Cathedral. It symbolizes the tree of life, as did the fruit trees of the Holy Land.

Page 52

Poppy (*Papaver*) bud stems nod, then straighten into colorful blossoms in the wildflower meadow along the Pilgrim Road.

Page 54

Oak trees spread their branches towards the peak of St. Alban's parish church. Established in 1854, the church was consecrated debt-free one year later with the help of funds left by Miss Phoebe Nourse, who had worshiped in the school chapel. Miss Nourse was the granddaughter of Joseph Nourse, Registrar of the Treasury, who had purchased what is now the 57-acre Cathedral close in 1813 and named it Mt. Saint Alban after his home in England.

Page 56

Tulips and Spanish bluebells (*Scilla hispanica*) star in the upper perennial border before the perennials come into their own.

Page 58

A twelfth-century Norman arch graces the entrance to the Bishop's Lawn from the Norman Court. It is flanked by two Atlas blue cedars (*Cedrus atlantica 'Glauca'*) brought from the Holy Land in 1901 and planted as foot-tall saplings.

Page 60

Icy strands of winterberry (*Ilex verticillata*) festoon the Robert C. Morton Border in early January.

Page 62

The *Cercis canadensis 'Alba,'* a white version of the American redbud, radiates heavenward along the Pilgrim Road.

Page 64

Native perennials of blue adorn the lower perennial border in late summer and early fall along the path to the Shadow House.

Page 66

A clump of snowdrops (*Galanthus nivalis*) nestles among the roots of an oak tree. Also known as Candlemas Bells, these fragrant flowers were often the subject of early Christian legends.

Page 68

The oakleaf hydrangea (*Hydrangea quercifolia*) growing in the border of the Bishop's Lawn forms an interesting pattern. This is a native American plant discovered by William Bartram during his travels in the Carolinas, Georgia, and Florida from 1773-1778. He wrote, "I observed here a very singular and beautiful shrub, which I suppose is a species of Hydrangea. The leaves...very much resemble the leaves of some of our Oaks..."

Page 70

A winter hush settles over the woodland. The wayfarer may seek shelter upon the roofed platform of the Japanese bridge.

Page 72

An azalea bud springs forth along the Woodland Path.

Page 74

The west facade of the Cathedral glows at sunset through a veil of oak trees that have stood for more than two centuries.

Page 76

"They shall enter into peace that enter in at these gates" is inscribed on the top bar of the gates at the Pilgrim Steps entrance to the Bishop's Garden. Designed and executed for this spot by Samuel Yellin of Philadelphia (1886-1940), they stand as a testament to the timeless work of this master blacksmith.

Page 78

The garth (medieval enclosed garden) on the north side of the Cathedral is a cloister garden with fountain. The native flowering dogwood (*Cornus Florida 'Rubra'*), under cultivation in this country since the early 1700's, robes itself in Easter finery.

Page 80

The gray skies of autumn reflect in the silvery ribbon of water that flows beneath the Japanese Bridge along the Woodland Path.

Page 82

This medieval garden "room" features a rose bed designed by Frederick Law Olmsted, Jr., and the granite statue of the Prodigal Son by Heinz Warneke. Boxwood, brick pathways, and a teak memorial bench complete the furnishings.

Page 84

A shimmering veil of water cools the garth (medieval enclosed garden) and its many visitors in midsummer. This contemporary bronze fountain completes the cloister garden planted and dedicated in 1969.

Page 86

Young girls of National Cathedral School cavort beneath the golden leaves of the shagbark hickory (*Carya ovata*) on the north lawn of the Cathedral.

Page 88

Lily-flowered 'White triumphator' tulips, Darwin 'Queen of Bartigons' tulips, and white-flowering quince surround the Wayside Cross in the upper perennial border of the Bishop's Garden. The Latin inscription encircling this ancient Celtic cross reads, *"Our souls are humbled even unto dust."* A survivor of the early days of the Christian faith, IHS is a transliteration of the Greek letters that spell Jesus, and are said to stand for "in this (cross) is salvation."

Page 90

The warm glow of Christmas shines through a Gothic window of the Herb Cottage, casting its spell over the snow-laden world of the fig and fringe trees.